MW01181178

Becoming Enabled:

A Busy Minister's Guide to Making the Gospel Accessible.

To all my disabled brothers and sisters and their families:

God sees you and He affirms your value. You are loved, empowered, and indispensable to the body of Christ. We need you; please don't give up on us. The Church is growing in its understanding, and we will continue. There are so many voices advocating for you; take heart.

To the pastor or volunteer reading this:

With utmost gratitude, I thank you. Thank you for caring. Thank you for trying. Thank you for seeing families like mine and affirming their value. I am so grateful and cannot wait to hear how this book affects your ministries.

For my boys:

I love you. The world will try to change you, but remember in whose image you are made. If I could go back and start all over, I still would choose, without hesitation, to have you.

For Cymber:

Sister, sister: I love you. You will never read these words, but one day when you reach Heaven, I hope you will smile ever so briefly knowing how much I love you. How much your life has changed the world because you have changed me. I would not be me without you.

Introduction

Chapter 1: The Biblical Backing for
Special Needs Ministry

Chapter 2: Get in Here!

Chapter 3: The Woo Factor

Chapter 4: In This Together

Chapter 5: Jumping the Hurdles

Chapter 6: Pastoring the Disabled

Chapter 7: Empowering the Disabled

Chapter 8: Closing Words

Chapter 9: Helpful Hacks

For, "everyone who calls on the name of the Lord will be saved."
How, then, can they call on the one they have not believed in?
And how can they believe in the one of whom they have not
heard? And how can they hear without someone preaching to
them? And how can anyone preach unless they are sent? As it is
written: "How beautiful are the feet of those who bring good
news!" – Romans 10:13-15 (NLT)

Dear readers,

I can only imagine what led you to pick up this book. Maybe you are a parent of children with special needs. Maybe you have a church home where your children are accepted and desire that for more children. Maybe you are a pastor and someone in your church has suggested that a ministry like this is needed in your church. Maybe you just see the need. Maybe God has called you to special needs ministry. Whatever brings you here, welcome! The heart of this book is to answer all the questions, from the theological backing for special needs ministry to how to start a ministry for your church.

Thank you. Thank you for following God's calling on your life. Thank you for being willing to serve Him. Thank you for caring about one of the most underserved people groups in the Church. There is a mission field in our backyard. We have an entire community of untapped giftings waiting to hear the good news. This community is vibrant, loyal, fun, and powerful. I implore you not to write off special needs ministry until you have read through the information in this book. Your church will grow in more than numbers, but also in faith and grace. You will not regret it. I am so excited to share this ministry God laid on my heart!

In Christ,

Joanna French

Special Needs Ministry
spesh-uhl needz **min**-uh-stree

---

noun
1. A ministry to persons affected by
   physical, mental, developmental
   or emotional disabilities
2. Binding up the broken hearted
3. Being a light in a dark place
4. Empowering the body to serve

Show It to Me:

The Biblical Backing for Special Needs Ministry.

Ministry is something you do. It's not lackadaisical or nonchalant. As ministry leaders, we do life with people and reach them where they are to share the gospel. This is true across all facets of ministry. People are reached in many different ways. For some it's going to be the community events your church does; for others it will be your worship team; still others will connect with your online presence. Those are just three examples of ways to reach people. These routes will also be what helps lead families of special needs children/adults to Christ. However, this is not the main requirement; to them there is something much more important, and it lines up with what Jesus did. They need to see their entire family is accepted as inherently valuable. If you cannot accept them all, you will win the hearts of none of them.

Most special needs families have an incredible bond. Parents are warriors for their children. Siblings, from a young age, become both advocates and helpers to their siblings. These families are fiercely loyal. Jo's story really brings home the point.

Jo was a Christian – well – "ish." Her faith had been tried heavily by life. She believed, yes, but it didn't really impact her. Not how it should have. She read the Bible maybe once a month, prayed when she needed something, and tried to be a good person.

Jo and her husband had two sons with autism. Her boys were the light of her life. They had just received their diagnoses when this thought crossed Jo's mind, *"The boys are going to need a community who loves them. I am going to need help from people who know how to raise these boys. I do not know how to help them."* So, Jo took her boys to church. The church, while well meaning, did not know how to handle her children's needs and showed little interest in learning. They told her, with looks of regret on their faces, "We would love to have you back, but you will need to leave your kids at home. We are not able to handle such disabled children."

Jo walked away and didn't walk back into another church until she moved back home two years later. Her faith was shaken. Her mental health spiraled. She felt alone during those two years. But Jo recovered. Her boys recovered. I am sorry to say her husband still, seven years later, has not. Raised in the church, he dove into the magical world of video games, where no one is disabled, no one is judgmental, and those who share your faith can't stab you in the back.

Jo's story is not an isolated one. Throughout the book, we will talk about several families who have similar stories. Maybe their children were allowed to exist in the church, but they were viewed as broken or possessed. There is a great deal of misunderstanding regarding what the Bible says about people with special needs and mental illness. We will address those struggles here. Worry not, we will hear more stories throughout these pages. There are many vibrant, funny, amazing adults and children with disabilities to meet.

Here are the facts: you will not find the term 'special needs ministry' in the Bible. You also won't find the term 'youth ministry' in the Bible. But no one questions if youth need the gospel. Somehow, one of the first questions I am asked by fellow pastors is, "But where do you find that in the Bible?"

My answer is simple: it's everywhere. It's in the fabric of the Word. It's just not written in neon lights. Maybe that's because God knows neon lights are both loud and bright enough to cause a meltdown. Who am I to say? But it's in there.

For God so loved the world that he gave his one and only Son, that whoever believes in him shall not perish but have eternal life. – John 3:16 NIV

      This is a scripture that even many atheists know. It is on T-shirts, wall art, coffee cups, and so many other items. Christians can live their entire lives surrounded by this scripture and miss the point. Jesus made it clear that day, talking to Nicodemus, who God loved. Let me tell you what Jesus didn't say:

- "God so loved the abled."
- "God so loved the religious."
- "God so loved the wise."
- "God so loved the quiet in church."
- "God so loved the comfortable."
- "God so loved the normal people."

No. He said plain as day that God so loved the *world*.

Christ not only died for all: he died for each.

Billy Graham

      I recognize there are two schools of thought on the "Is Jesus God?" question. I wholeheartedly believe Jesus is fully God. I see God coming to Earth, living a spotless life as a man, being mistreated and abused, then killed, and rising again. What incredible love that shows!

      When God loved the world, He did not love only the normal people, the quiet people, or the people who fit into a cookie cutter. He loved us all with an incredible love that is unfathomable by human standards.

Can you imagine how it must grieve God's heart that His church isn't doing everything it can to bring others to Him? Can you imagine? Jesus was mocked, falsely accused, beaten, whipped, and hung on the cross so the world would have access to the gospel. I assure you, it is not His heart that we leave anyone untold.

Moses said to the Lord, "Pardon your servant, Lord. I have never been eloquent, neither in the past nor since you have spoken to your servant. I am slow of speech and tongue." The Lord said to him, "Who gave human beings their mouths? Who makes them deaf or mute? Who gives them sight or makes them blind? Is it not I, the Lord? – Exodus 4:10-11 NIV

As he went along, he saw a man blind from birth. His disciples asked him, "Rabbi, who sinned, this man or his parents, that he was born blind?" "Neither this man nor his parents sinned," said Jesus, "but this happened so that the works of God might be displayed in him. – John 9:1-3 NIV

Maybe you hadn't realized it, but right there in the book of Exodus, God makes it clear that He intentionally makes people deaf, blind, and mute. I add the caveat that I don't believe He would have before the fall. Our God works with what is to make Himself tangible to His people. Moses questioned his usefulness, but God – oh, God! – saw it from the first.

I paired these scriptures together because I love the continuity of the Bible. God makes people deaf, blind, and mute. You don't have to have some grave sin involved to be born that way. Sometimes, and I would argue more often than not, this happens, "...so that the works of God might be displayed in..." their lives. What a beautiful picture.

God is intentional. He doesn't do happenstance. So when a child is born different from the norm, God is not surprised. These atypical people have a unique gift to give the world and a unique offering to give God. Often, their light shines more brightly, their sacrifices are given more freely, their joy is unencumbered.

When Jesus said, "...let the little children come to me, for the kingdom of God belongs to those such as these," he was talking about childlike faith. The kind of faith our brothers and sisters with disabilities actually have the upper hand in possessing. Disability is not a surprise. God doesn't come up with a contingency plan just in case a person is born with a disability or becomes disabled later in life. He sees it coming, and He prepares a good work in them, knowing what lies ahead.

For it is by grace you have been saved, through faith—and this is not from yourselves, it is a gift from God—not by works, so that no one can boast. For we are God's handiwork, created in Christ Jesus to do good works, which God prepared in advance for us to do. – Ephesians 2:8-10 NIV

Three times I pleaded with the Lord to take it away from me. But he said to me, "My grace is sufficient for you, for my power is made perfect in weakness." Therefore, I will boast all the more gladly about my weaknesses, so that Christ's power may rest on me. That is why, for Christ's sake, I delight in weaknesses, in insults, in hardships, in persecutions, in difficulties. For when I am weak, then I am strong. – 2 Corinthians 12:8-10 NIV

"So that no one can boast," and, "Therefore, I will boast all the more gladly about my weaknesses...for when I am weak, then I am strong." These scriptures go hand in hand. We cannot boast of our worth of grace we've received. But if we boast, let us boast in our weaknesses. If God be glorified by them, then to God be the glory always.

Ephesians 2:10 is our key scripture for Flint Hills Embrace—the special needs ministry I founded in our church nearly six years ago. We wholeheartedly believe that God's beautiful workmanship can be found in the image of all people, including the disabled.

Never have I seen purer worship than when our friend Colton would sing and dance at church. He knows his Savior in a way many would covet. He really *knows* Jesus. Colton worships in the throne room of God every Sunday, as he has no earthly chains that could keep him from meeting with God. Nothing keeps him bound here. I don't know how to explain it, but you can see it. Colton is non-verbal. He has never spoken a word, but God hears him clearly.

God created in Colton a worshiper. Our people got to see him meet with God every Sunday, which made many seek to dive deeper in their own relationship with God. Colton is also a natural encourager. His smile and excitement light up even the darkest rooms. These are his good works. These are the things he brings to our church. They are beautiful.

Colton and his mom moved six months ago, and our church has not been the same without them. Both of their absences are felt deeply. Because of their presence, our church was changed. Oh, we miss them so much!

Now if the foot should say, "Because I am not a hand, I do not belong to the body," it would not for that reason stop being part of the body. And if the ear should say, "Because I am not an eye, I do not belong to the body," it would not for that reason stop being part of the body. If the whole body were an eye, where would the sense of hearing be? If the whole body were an ear, where would the sense of smell be? But in fact God has placed the parts in the body, every one of them, just as he wanted them to be. If they were all one part, where would the body be? As it is, there are many parts, but one body. The eye cannot say to the hand, "I don't need you!" And the head cannot say to the feet, "I don't need you!" On the contrary, those parts of the body that seem weaker are indispensable...Now you are the body of Christ, and each one of you is a part of it

– I Corinthians 12:15-22, 27 NIV

We need each other. Oh, we so desperately need each other! Proverbs tells us as iron sharpens iron so one person sharpens another. This is not the season to be dull. The gospel has always been counter-cultural. I think we can agree it has become increasingly more so in our world. We *cannot* be dull. We cannot pretend not to need each other. Our church has seen something incredible since the start of our special needs ministry years ago. I couldn't say it better than one of my precious friends who volunteers with Embrace.

Embrace has changed our church by making us more than hearers of the word, but doers. It has clearly set the precedence that all are made in God's image and have a place in God's kingdom. Special needs ministry in our church has shattered the idea that we should all conform to the same mold and encourages us to embrace God's creative diversity in the church.

Lisa Bowers, ministry volunteer.

Yes, brothers and sisters, those parts of the body that seem weaker are actually indispensable.

It is my belief that you have not seen the most beautiful things the church has to offer until you have worshipped alongside a nonverbal adult who rocks before the Lord because they are filled with so much joy they cannot sit still. I have seen an echo of myself and my Savior in the eyes of a child after a huge behavioral struggle; he looked up at me to ask, "Do you still love me? How can you still love me?" Serving those whom the world deems useless is priceless.

People go into special needs ministry with the priority to do something to help others, and they are. But what of the way these precious brothers and sisters will shore up *your* faith? That, my friends, is without measure. We need each other. We need to encourage one another. The church is not complete without our brothers and sisters with disabilities. When men and women, young and old, abled and disabled, worship and grow together, the body of Christ comes alive. When this happens, we can effectively reflect the love of our Savior. God, in His infinite wisdom, knew we would need each other and gifted us all.

And Mephibosheth lived in Jerusalem, because he always ate at the king's table; he was lame in both feet. – II Samuel 9:13 NIV

Oh, the story of Mephibosheth. It is one of my very favorites. Here is David, a man after God's own heart, inviting Mephibosheth to join him and eat at his own table. Mephibosheth was the grandson of King Saul, the man who spent years trying to kill David. The other kings around him would have had Mephibosheth killed, but not David.

David, this incredible man after God's own heart, does something completely counter-cultural. He, the king, ensures not only that all of Mephibosheth's needs are met, but that he would eat with the king. This story tells us who is welcome at "The King's Table." All who would come.

Thank God this is true! I am so grateful for a God who embraces us no matter what is 'wrong' with us. I am a neurodivergent pastor who also has P.T.S.D. and a chronic illness. I have been praying in faith for years to be healed of the mental and physical plights I face. Alas, the response seems to be that His power is made clear in my weakness.

I am, like all of us, a genuine mess. I just happen to be messy in a unique way. Dare I say, if you were to talk to our lead pastor, he would tell you that working with me is not always easy: I am forgetful, a bit picky, need greater assistance than most people, and sometimes am highly emotional, but he will also tell you it is worth it. That our church is better because of me.

I hope you can hear how uncomfortable this is to say. I am not claiming I am somehow more integral than a person without a disability. Years of retraining my brain and seeing what God can do through me has taught me I am just as needed in the church as our lead pastor.

Your church needs people who are different. Who don't think and act the same. All churches do. How will they come though if they don't hear?

When one of those at the table with him heard this, he said to Jesus, "Blessed is the one who will eat at the feast in the kingdom of God. Jesus replied: "A certain man was preparing a great banquet and invited many guests. At the time of the banquet he sent his servant to tell those who had been invited, 'Come, for everything is now ready.' But they all alike began to make excuses. The first said, 'I have just bought a field, and I must go and see it. Please excuse me.' Another said, 'I have just bought five yoke of oxen, and I'm on my way to try them out. Please excuse me.' Still another said, 'I just got married, so I can't come.' The servant came back and reported this to his master. Then the owner of the house became angry and ordered his servant, 'Go out quickly into the streets and alleys of the

town and bring in the poor, the crippled, the blind and the lame.'
'Sir,' the servant said, 'what you ordered has been done, but
there is still room.' Then the master told his servant, 'Go out to
the roads and country lanes and compel them to come in, so
that my house will be full. I tell you, not one of those who were
invited will get a taste of my banquet.' " – Luke 14:15-24 NIV

We know Jesus' parables were told to teach a lesson. While not entirely literal, they were entirely intentional. It's not a difficult thing to assume we were intentionally being instructed to invite others into the Lord's banquet. The poor, the crippled, the blind, the lame; these people were not the elite in society. They were the outcasts. They were the ones who were not wanted. They were the people everyone assumed God had just cursed. But Jesus said bring them in.

You know how I know for sure that this is what Jesus was saying? Because his words were a response to a statement: "Blessed is the one who will eat at the feast in the kingdom of God."

Both literally and figuratively, the kingdom of God is going to welcome the misfits. The broken. The unwanted. The invisible. The quiet. The last choice for everyone else is who God picks as his 'A team.'

Don't believe me? Look at the disciples. I am not saying they were disabled, but they were not traditional disciple material. They were misfits. God has a heart for the broken, the lost, the disabled, and yes, the misfits. Why? Because they are humble. They are receptive. They recognize how little they can bring to God and yet God says that's exactly what I want. Your church is not fulfilling its God-given commands if it's not welcoming all these people. The disabled are just one group of these people.

Therefore, go and make disciples of all nations, baptizing them in the name of the Father, and the Son, and the Holy Spirit, and teaching them to obey everything I have commanded you. And surely I am with you always, to the very end of the age.

– Matthew 28: 19-20 NIV

Who doesn't love the Great Commission? We regularly use it to explain why missions is so important. We have already established that Jesus died so that all could hear, so why mention this scripture? Because it comes with a promise: when we go and teach, we are promised He will be with us always. This is a promise that as you prayerfully and thoughtfully give your all to reach people, He will be with you always. This is worth mentioning because – apart from Him being with us – I daresay no ministry goals could be effectively accomplished.

Casting Crowns recently released a song called *Start Right Here*. It speaks to this very issue when it says:

> We want our blessings in our pockets
> We keep our missions overseas
> But for the hurting in our cities
> Would we even cross the street?

The American church is right to care about those in remote lands who have never heard about the gospel. But we have to stop overlooking those in our own backyard who either have not heard the gospel or do not understand it. To many, the church feels like an exclusive club, and this is a shame. I cannot encourage you enough that we are to tell all. When we are not willing to do this, the church itself becomes disabled.

To put it in perspective, here is a brief synopsis of disability ministry theology condensed in one place.

◇ When God loved the world, he loved us all.

- God created us all, and He did so with intentionality. Some of us, He created 'normal,' but some He created intentionally with disability. Disability is no surprise to God.
- We are all God's handiwork, and He can use us all as we are. Through our weaknesses, His glory is shown.
- The church needs us all – abled and not. We sharpen each other and make each other's faith stronger.
- We know there is a place at God's table for all who would come, and God seeks for all to be made right with Him.
- Therefore, it is the Church's job to GO and make disciples of all people, the disabled included.

The body of Christ simply is not complete without these families. They are created with gifts the church needs. They and their families are souls that need Christ.

The next logical question is: why don't they just attend church? Let's explore that question next.

Why Don't They Come?

I think a logical place to start is to consider what types of disability your church could face. Disability comes in many forms, and you can have multiple people with multiple types of disabilities. Here are three main categories:

- **Physical:** A physical disability is a disability that impacts a person physically. It may affect a person's mobility, stamina, or fine motor skills. Common physical disabilities include muscular dystrophy and spina bifida.
- **Developmental:** A developmental disability is characterized by a significant developmental delay. These disabilities tend to be lifelong. This is the largest category, as it can envelop physical disabilities as well as intellectual disabilities (i.e. a person with a lower-than-average IQ.) Some common developmental disabilities include autism and Down syndrome.
- **Emotional:** An emotional disability is one that affects a person's ability to recognize, interpret, and effectively express emotions in an appropriate way. These disabilities can lead to anger outbursts and tears. Common emotional disabilities include bipolar disorder, anxiety, and depression.

A person can have one or multiple disabilities from one category, or they can have diagnoses from all three.

The same person can be diagnosed with both Down syndrome and autism. Autism is often co-morbid with ADHD and depression. Illnesses that are primarily physical, like Sanfilippo syndrome, can cause developmental delays over time.

Special needs ministry is a newer ministry in today's churches. For a very long time, people actually believed that disabilities were a punishment from God. We have established this is simply not the case.

I have a dear friend whose fabulous boy, Micah, is now 19. He has autism and is considered classically low functioning. But he's not. He is smart and introverted. Sometimes he has behavioral struggles. He is always a good, funny, kind young man who just needs space to flourish.

Micah's mom told me of her struggles with attending church when he was younger. People would invite her to church, insisting their congregation welcomes all. After attending once, the invitation would be quickly retracted. They were not willing to deal with his type of behavioral issues.

As Micah has gotten older, he still struggles in social situations. He gets easily overwhelmed. When he attended our church once, he hit a brand-new guest. The guest responded perfectly; he laughed it off and joked about getting pizza with him. "You have to be a bro to hit me like that," he said. That's one of my favorite things: our church's culture has a wonderfully laid-back attitude about things like that.

Micah's mom has been taught by society her child doesn't fit in. That's a challenging hurdle for her to overcome. We learn from experience, and experience taught my friend that her child was not welcome in church.

She worries every time they come to church, even to this day. Will he break something? Will he hurt someone? Will people be offended he doesn't get involved? Will he feel judged or unwanted? Will I? These fears are valid in the disability community when it comes to leaving the safety of their home. People whose lives are shaped by disability often struggle to be in public for many reasons.

There is a consistent checklist of questions that go through their minds:

- Will my child be able to handle all the sensory input there?
- Will they accept my family?
- What if my child has a meltdown? How will the people react?
- Will my child be able to use their wheelchair accessible features? Do they even have wheelchair access?
- How will my child react to the other children?
- Will the kids understand and be kind?

This is just a small list that runs through the minds of special needs parents.

Did you know that one person in four has a disability? That fact is staggering. 25% of our population has a physical, mental, developmental, or behavioral impaction. If the church ignores these people, what happens? 25% of our population doesn't come to know Christ. That's on the low side, actually.

Remember, those with disabilities have parents, siblings, spouses, and children. So many people's lives are affected by disability, the shock wave felt by their lack of presence in the Kingdom will be disastrous, and we will be held accountable for our apathy.

Often, but not always, those whose lives are impacted by disability weigh a long list of pros and cons, live in survival mode, and decide church is just not worth the energy or the risk. We have to be willing to help families break these cycles. The church should be the easiest place to feel wanted and accepted.

Micah's mom doesn't attend church now. But do you know what the coolest thing is? He does! He joins us online about every other Sunday. Sometimes, while I am preaching or giving announcements, he will text me, "Hi, Joanna." His mom gets to hear him sing the worship music. She sees him being involved and invested in the way he is able. Who knows, maybe it will bring her to church one day. Maybe it won't. Honestly, my hope is that it brings her to the Lord, whether or not that be at our church.

When my children were little, they were not welcome in grocery stores without judgement. Seriously, I remember going to a little store down the road from us and shopping for five or six things. Jairmie, my oldest who has autism, was in the cart; he was happy, humming and rocking. I was blocked by a very disgruntled man who looked down at my beautiful boy, glared back up at me, rolled his eyes and said, "The world would be better if kids like him were put down."

This is probably the most extreme statement I have heard. Jairmie will be eleven years old soon. He is kind, funny, and in love with God. He wants to be baptized and asked me if he could. I told him that was between him and God, and I encouraged him to pray about it. While delayed in almost all other ways he could be, he can stand independently in spiritual matters. He knows the voice of God. So I told him to take it up with God. He came back an hour later; after swinging and praying on the swing in our backyard.

"I am happy/sad. I am happy God wants me to be on team Jesus always, but sad 'cuz he told me I'm not ready yet. He said I wouldn't be ready till I was 12 or 13. I have to read my Bible more. I have to understand God more. How do I get ready, Mom?"

I can promise you, the world certainly would be worse if he were not in it. What a warrior for Christ it would lose!

When they had finished eating, Jesus said to Simon Peter, "Simon son of John, do you love me more than these?"

"Yes, Lord," he said, "you know that I love you." Jesus said, "Feed my lambs." Again, Jesus said, "Simon son of John, do you love me?" He answered, "Yes, Lord, you know that I love you." Jesus said, "Take care of my sheep." The third time he said to him, "Simon son of John, do you love me?" Peter was hurt because Jesus asked him the third time, "Do you love me?" He said, "Lord, you know all things; you know that I love you." Jesus said, "Feed my sheep." – John 21:15-17 NIV

I want to ask you the same question: do you love Him? How, then, can you ignore His sheep? Our Savior is the kind that would leave the ninety-nine for the one. Surely, He would go after the 25%.

Okay, Joanna, but where do we start?

I suppose that depends on your church culture. There are some simple ways any church can begin to take small steps toward becoming enabled.

1. Have a monthly prayer focus for those with mental illness/physical disabilities. Do not focus your prayers on healing; this can be hurtful and cause stumbling. After all, sometimes God says no. Instead focus them on things like hope, joy, and friendship. Thank God for their giftings. Pray consistently for their families, too. Pray God's will for them. Ask God to give them strength.

2. Hold a growth training focused on disability. I have done these at churches, and I know many other special needs pastors who would love to step in and assist you in leading this type of training. These can also be done over online platforms, which is pretty cool!

3. Have a quiet space and sensory bags ready for those with disabilities. Please know that many kids with disabilities focus better when fidgeting. What used to be considered rude is found to improve the absorption

of information and memory. Common items for a sensory bag include:

- ◇ Noise canceling headphones (for sound sensitivity)
- ◇ Squishy fidgets, fidget spinners
- ◇ Coloring sheets and crayons
- ◇ Etch-A-Sketch or marble maze games
- ◇ Weighted lap pads

4. Make your church service is available online. This does two things: it shares the gospel with those who won't or can't leave home, and it gives those who want to venture out a clear picture of your church's typical service.
5. Talk to a disabled family; ask what would make church more feasible for them. Then take action to make it happen.

These are five simple places to become more intentional. Starting here is doable for any church. It will naturally grow!

Make sure you begin to share the message that you want to worship with the disabled. The scriptures listed in the previous section would be a fabulous teaching series to introduce your church to the idea of intentionally welcoming all.

Please understand that welcoming the disabled is not an overnight venture. These families have been burned by people time and again. They have been rejected. Some parents are angry that God would allow their child to be disabled. What kind of a loving God wants my kids to suffer? They may ask questions like this. We will discuss this situation later; for now, the most important question to ask is this: how do we get these people to come to our church so we can show them how loved they are?

For that, friends, we have to take this show on the road.

The Woo Factor

Have you ever noticed that Jesus met people where they were, without fail? He never said, "Meet me at the temple in Jerusalem. We will talk there." No. He met the people where the people were.

At a well.

On the shores of the Sea of Galilee.

In the streets.

He met them where they were. He also met the needs of those who would seek Him. He fed them. He healed them. He listened to them. He respected them. Our approach to ministry, across the board, must be the same. We were not meant to be stuck in holy huddles. We were made to be rivers, not puddles.

Oops. It looks like my love of poetry is coming out. The fact is, we were given the Gospel first to live, then to share. In this chapter, we will discuss both approaches.

Meeting them where they are: Let's take this show on the road.

Where do you find the disabled? Oof. This is a loaded question: technically, the answer is all around you. But how do you meet them in an environment where it feels like them, like it's their territory? Where they feel invincible?

Friends, there are so many options, but I *will* share with you that it takes some very creative thinking. Special needs ministry will work the 'out of the box' thinking muscle in your brain. Here are a few ideas, some simple, others a little more complicated. You can fit them to what your church can do.

1. Reach out to your congregation. It's likely someone in your congregation has friends, or even family, with a disability. Learn from them. Be

straightforward. How can we better welcome those with disabilities? What are we doing right? How can we do better? Asking these questions, and others, will help them feel heard and valued!

2. Partner with your local library to do a read-aloud for the disabled population. It doesn't even need to be a faith-based book. Doctor Suess will work just fine. Do this monthly. Form connections. Get to know the families who come. Remember their names. Pray for them. Eventually they will ask you what you do, and you can say, "I am a pastor at xyz church here in town." These relationships will develop naturally. A word of wisdom. I would always make sure you have both a male and female volunteer. If dads come, they can feel comfortable talking to a man, and moms may feel safer talking to another woman.

3. Serve water for the local Special Olympics. Go to tournaments. Celebrate their victories and compliment them on their efforts when they lose. Have pizza parties for the kids of the Special Olympics (offer several types of pizza including gluten-friendly and cheese only, food sensitivities and allergies are common in this population).

4. If your church is large enough, host a "Night to Shine" event. If not, volunteer at one in your area. Not only will you have the best time ever, but you will make connections with these families.

5. Give a gift to the local developmental center. Hygiene products, craft supplies, and so many other things could be a huge blessing. Cash donations are also greatly appreciated. Recognizing what these people do and forming relationships with them could open the door for future Bible studies and

other ministry opportunities. After all, we are to go and make disciples without prejudice or selection.

6. Work with a local salon to host a sensory friendly hair cut day. The blessing this service offers in the special needs community would surprise you. Depending on the size of your town, this could be a full-day event or just a few hours. This cooperative event offers benefits to the families as well as the business. It also creates opportunities for relationship building and fosters a space for community education and involvement.

Once you do a few of these things, you are off to a great start, but there is more. You may have already started to see a few families trickle in. Now it's time to kick it up a notch!

Meeting the Needs (and wants) of Special Needs Families.

There are certain things we all need. Food, water, and shelter are typical requirements that come to mind when we consider need. Yet it goes much deeper than that. We need social interaction. We need rest. We need to recharge. We need a group of people that are 'our people.' These are some of the needs that severely lack within the disability community.

I remember when my son was only six months old. I was on day three of him not sleeping. I don't mean he would only sleep a couple hours and then was up. I mean, for some reason, he could not fall sleep. I went to the doctor, and they determined he was not producing the right amount of melatonin. He was crying endlessly. His brain was tired. His body needed rest, too. But he could not sleep. That also meant that I could not sleep.

In this stage of our marriage, my husband was working eight hours a day and going to school six more hours. After that exhausting schedule, he would promptly come home and fall asleep. He needed to sleep. He needed to be able to care for us. But in that 72-hour period, I think I must have slept for about two hours, tops. I was exhausted, I cried over everything, and the tiredness made me sick. I was emotional and impatient.

Sitting in that doctor's office, I cried and tried to comfort my Jairmie. Desperately, I tried to comfort him. I wept and sang, "I love you, a bushel and a peck, and a hug around the neck. A barrel and a heap and I'm talking in my sleep *incoherent sobs*." The doctor told us to go pick up melatonin and give that a try. He sympathized, but until we used his advice, there wasn't much more he could do.

This is not an isolated event. I know many special needs children that simply don't believe in sleep. I don't know why, but they just don't. It's like they can effectively function on one or two hours of sleep when the rest of us need six to eight. This creates a void. Let us assess my situation, shall we? What difference could a church family have made?

Could a church family have made my child sleep? No, they could not. But...

Could a church family have given me a little reprieve to sleep? Yes, they could! Could they have encouraged me? Yes. Could they have reminded me I was not alone? Yes.

But I didn't have a church family. It was clear that my Jairmie and I were not welcome in church. He cried endlessly, which became a problem. I know now the lights hurt him. Not the sight of them, but the sound of them. The church we attended had long fluorescent lights, like the ones at Wal-Mart. They hurt him to this day. The lights emit a buzz that causes him discomfort, then pain. It's becoming less severe over time, though. He also had to be held by me in church, which was an issue because he didn't like being touched at this age. For these and other reasons, I wasn't welcome, and neither was my boy.

I sometimes wonder where I would be in my faith today if they had just loved us. No, I seriously do. I recognize it is not the pastor's responsibility to grow our faith, but it *is* the responsibility of the pastor to offer an environment in which we can grow. There is a difference.

My family was not offered this environment. I took that as a clear statement: since the church didn't want me, God didn't either. So yes, I sometimes wonder how I would be different, but I will never know the answer. The church can make a significant difference by accepting and welcoming those with disabilities and supporting the needs of parents and families. The need for rest. The need for friendship. And other basic needs.

Some special needs families have to miss work for days, weeks, or even months to take care of the medical needs of their children. This creates additional financial burdens. Maybe they will need help with gas to get to the hospital. Maybe they will need money for their electric bill. Maybe they will need food. Maybe they will need assistance with medically proactive childcare. Can your church help meet a need? Can you connect them with those who can?

Shifting gears ever so slightly, I want to talk to you a little bit about the special needs family. As precious and wonderful as our children are, they add a different type of stress. I am not interested in making comparisons. I am a firm believer that everyone's greatest pain is equal because it is the thing that hurt the most. We *all* have stress. As special needs parents, we are not exempt from all the stresses of typical parenthood. Conversely, parents of typical children may not experience the type of stresses we do.

Regardless, we will all eventually need support, and that fact is a great equalizer. Here's one of the differences you may see. Some families attend sports practice and art classes; our children are probably going to physical, occupational, or speech therapy. Even worse, they might not be welcomed at places where other kids socialize and interact. So we become isolated. We can't just get a teenager to babysit, so date nights and quality time are rare. This, coupled with additional mental, physical, and emotional strain, can lead to the collapse of the marriage.

Disclaimer: I hate this conversation. It makes my children look and sound like a burden. They are not. They are a blessing. They are a beautiful gift. All children, no matter their functioning level, are gifts. We love them. They bring us joy just like your children, but the church cannot bear the naivete that says, "Because you love them, it's easy." It isn't. It's hard.

The divorce rate among families with special needs children is astounding. Why? Because parents are too busy putting out fires. They become coworkers instead of lovers. They have to relegate their relationship to the back burner because their child needs them and no one can help. This is one of the most underserved needs the church can meet. We can help special needs families have time together.

I want to introduce you to the idea of a respite night. Respite simply means providing a break or rest to someone. Our church offers this event to care for special needs children (and non-impacted siblings) in a fun and safe environment so parents can go out on a date. Or shop. Or just rest.

At our church, respite nights are three hours long. That's all. But do you know what we have seen in three hours? Couples going to marriage counseling or going on dates, parents going to buy groceries, and even one parent sleeping out in the parking lot. All were grateful. So grateful. As a result of our respite program, we have also welcomed 11 families into our church!

How does this program work? We use a rotation system with activity stations to create an opportunity for controlled chaos. Respite nights need order and function, but you must be willing to be flexible to last minute changes. Our church is small and doesn't offer much space; you may be able to offer more or different stations, or you may have a completely different set-up.

1. We divide our sanctuary in half, creating two separate sections, one for a game and one for a craft. (See page on respite activities.)
2. Our basement children's area becomes the movie station.
3. We provide a sensory area in the foyer with a tent, a crash pad, and various sensory activities. (See page on sensory activities.)
4. Our sensory safe room (a quiet, safe space discussed later) is open and available for children who need it.

We have divided our kids into different groups for different seasons. When Covid-19 mandates were in effect, we created groups based on families. Siblings and close family friends were grouped together, masks were required for volunteers and recommended for children, and volunteers cleaned quickly between groups.

Now that requirements have lifted, we still offer masks and maintain cleaning, but we separate groups based on age rather than family. This allows younger children to pair together, it gives older siblings a chance to play and have fun, and we can offer a group for adults with disabilities so their parents or guardians can have a break, too. Each age group is designated with a color: 1- to 5-year-olds have red name tags, 6- to 10-year-old have blue, 11- to 14-year-olds have green, and 15-years and up have orange. They rotate through the stations in 45-minute increments.

Kids and volunteers eat dinner in their section halfway through the evening. We often have our youth group serve and clean up the meal, since they are not old enough to qualify as adult volunteers, but no one is ever too young to be valuable. Meals vary depending on the respite night and the budget allowances. However, simple is best. Some good choices we have served include hotdogs and macaroni and cheese or pizza and yogurt tubes. We offer fruit and veggies with every meal, taking into consideration the dietary needs of the children we welcome. If we have a child with allergies, food sensitivities, or other issues of note, we accommodate however we can. No matter what, we do not make any child eat what we offer. They choose for themselves.

One aspect of our ministry that is small but valuable is our gift bags. Each child who comes to a respite night receives a simple gift bag personalized with his or her name. They feel so special when they get to take a bag of goodies home with them. Our bags include:

1. A pencil
2. A fidget toy
3. A sticker
4. A notebook
5. Candy
6. A card from our church

Each of these gift bags cost the church about $1. They make a huge impact on these kids by helping them feel both loved and valued. It's just an example of how the smallest things have the ability to make a huge difference in ministry.

An important thing to do for respite night is to have families sign up in advance. We use Google forms, but you can use whatever platform that works best for you. Here is an example of one of the forms we require families to fill out online.

We currently have the ability to welcome 1 neurotypical sibling per impacted child. If we have further availability and can welcome more of your neurotypical children, you will be contacted no later than two days before respite night. Thank you for understanding.

Child 1

What is your name?

What is your phone number?

What is your child's name?

How old is your child?

What is your child's disability?

Does your child have food allergies? If so, what are they?

What are some techniques for comforting your child?

What is your email address?

Child 2

What is your child's name?

How old is your child?

What is your child's disability?

Does your child have food allergies? If so, what are they?

What are some techniques for comforting your child?

We are excited to spend time with your child and hope you enjoy your break! You deserve this! God Bless.

At the end of each respite, we are intentional about telling parents something that we appreciated about their children. This step allows parents to see someone else value their child, and it helps volunteers connect with their kids. We also tell the kids how much we have loved having them.

After respite night, there is one last important thing to do. Use their email address and reach out. Tell them thank you for coming and ask them about their experience. We have yet to receive a negative email. Everyone is grateful, and it can bring people to church over time. Which can bring them to Christ, and that is always the end goal.

Commit to hosting respite nights as often as is feasible for you. If it is a challenge to get enough volunteers, then ask another church to join. I know churches who do them every other week, and ones who do them once a year. Our church holds quarterly respite nights. We have a small church, which limits our budget and volunteer staff. Our set-up requires a minimum of 11 volunteers, which can be a challenge to staff because of our size.

Each section needs at least one permanent volunteer, and each group of children needs at least one volunteer, depending on group size, church size, and other local legal requirements for this type of event. During each rotation, each section should have at least three volunteers in total. You may also consider volunteers to help make, deliver, serve, or clean up the meal, youth volunteers as runners and one-to-one helpers for elopers, a security member if needed, and one or two floaters for the sensory safe room or helpers for diaper changes and toileting needs. These positions add up quickly, and you never want to burn out your volunteers.

Speaking of volunteer burnout, we always give volunteers a gift. These people must know you appreciate them.

It can be something small, simple, and 'punny.' A bag of popcorn that says, "Thanks for making our respite night pop," or a candy bar that says, "You make our ministry sweeter." Gestures like this make a vital impact on volunteer morale! (See page on volunteer appreciation gifts.)

Another program we love is our Mental Health Outreach. This is one any church can do! Our ministry commits to four outreaches per year. We spend about $100 a year making signs with positive, encouraging messages of hope. We stand on the sidewalks of one of the local parks and hold our signs to show community members that someone cares for them. We hold an outreach on Valentine's Day, Veteran's Day, and two other days around May and August.

The signs have messages that read, "The world is better with you in it," "You are welcome and wanted here," "Keep shining," "It's okay not to be okay," and other encouraging phrases. We also have signs that say, "Thank you for your service," and "22 a day is 22 too many," in response to the veterans and the military members in our community. We usually get about 10-20 people to hold up signs and share love.

We have had people come into our church and say, "I was planning on killing myself until I saw your sign, thank you." This outreach has also brought new members to our church because they wanted to serve somewhere they could help people with mental illness.

Although mental illness will not be as consistently discussed as developmental disabilities, I must make it clear that mental illnesses can be just as impactful. They can be just as painful. These families need our love and support just as much as any other family.

There are many other options available to meet the needs of the disabled/mentally ill.

- Family nights (movies, crafts, etc.)
- Seasonal events (summer-water activities, fall-festivals, etc.)
- Family photos
- Inclusive sensory safe worship experience
- Adults with developmental disabilities small groups
- Image based kids' curriculum
- Weekly phone calls

It may seem complicated; I promise, if my church can do it, yours can, too. And you will not regret it.

Supporting Your Community Champions

I want to make a statement that should be obvious to all churches, but we still miss it. WE are to be Jesus to the world. We are to reflect the love of our Savior. Jesus didn't just commune in the temple, He served in the streets, ministering there as well. WE must do the same. We must go out in our community, work with them, love on them, and share with them The Good News!

Once you decide to get started, you will have much that can be learned from professionals who already work with adults and children with disabilities. They have hard jobs. As meaningful, beautiful, and wonderful as their work is, they have hard jobs. Unfortunately, their jobs are also often thankless. So who are these professionals to whom you should look for wisdom? There are so many possibilities:

- Doctors and Nurses: They understand the physical side of the disability world.
- Therapists: Speech and language pathologists know how to help children communicate more effectively and how you can more effectively communicate with them. Occupational therapists can help you understand how to plan for people with fine motor deficiencies in your church. They can also help you integrate sensory learning into children's lessons, which can help all children retain information better. Physical therapists will be able to help you learn to use the equipment some of your buddies may need. They can also help you be a positive part of their growth. Finally, psychological therapists can give you window into the emotional, hidden reasons children may be struggling and how to be a support to these children and their parents.
- Special Education Teachers: They understand the educational needs of special needs persons.

- Paraprofessionals: They understand how to implement these needs (they are the many hands of a teacher who cannot be 100 places at once.)
- Local Developmental Centers: Children with disabilities grow up to be adults with disabilities. By partnering with your local developmental center, you will open doors to working with adults who may be unable to live independently. This can be done easily as we will discuss shortly.
- Developmental Pediatrician (DP): These people are diagnosticians. Having a good relationship with a couple of DPs will prove helpful when a member of your church comes to you with the question, "Is my child disabled?" This will happen; trust me. Having a referral contact allows you to say, "I am not qualified to diagnose your child, but I understand your concerns and encourage you to contact Lacey Stacey at DP, Inc." This ability will be a huge help to you. It will help the parent feel heard without requiring you to answer questions you're not qualified to answer.

Each and every one of these professionals is a person God adores. They are a person for whom Jesus died. It is an honor to reflect the Savior to them. It is a blessing to see how, saved or lost, we can see God's image in them. We are all image bearers, and these men and women reflect that in such a precious, unique way.

How do I form these connections?

You may already have a few of these people as members of your church. Connecting with others in your community starts with one thing: gratitude. Gratitude is the most effective way I have found to make an impact and a contact simultaneously.

Let me give you some examples of how we formed connections with each of the above. These strategies are interchangeable. What can you afford? A thank you card is better than most professionals in these fields get. We also consider how much time they need to spend with impacted children and families. Let God lead you as you decide. The Holy Spirit will not lead you astray. Here are some ideas.

Doctors and Nurses: Thank you cards to local pediatricians. Attach a mini-candy bar. We give these gifts yearly. It costs us roughly $5 for 20 people.

Therapists: Thank you gift bags, containing a few treats, a fidget, and a pen. We give these gifts once a quarter. This costs us roughly $35 for 30 people.

Special Education Teachers (and paras): We give this group an annual Christmas gift, comprised of one small gift for each special education teacher, para, and therapist in our school district. We have given handcrafted items and small gift bags. Our most recent bag included a winter ruler, a mini-Christmas

Pro-Tip

Shop sales. I am 100% serious. We shop online to buy items for the school district Christmas gift in January, when Christmas notebooks are deeply discounted. Shop for school supplies during back-to-school sales and store them. You can save around 70% like this. Look for items you want to keep stocked the same way. If you have never been a sale shopper, I promise you have some in your congregation. Find them!

notebook, and a few pieces of candy. Each school in our district also receives 1-2 boxes of school supplies for their special education classrooms. This is our most extravagant gift. We spend an annual average of $450 for around 400 professionals and 25 boxes of school supplies.

Local Developmental Center: Once a year, we take a gift to our local developmental center. We include crafting supplies like markers, paints, coloring books, and crayons. We also include hygiene products. Because these centers have live-in residents, they need supplies for daily life. This is a huge way to be a blessing to adults with disabilities. It could even open a pathway to Bible study opportunities.

Developmental Pediatricians: Heart felt thank you card and a small basket of goodies for their office. We did this one time, spent $25, and now we receive phone calls asking about our respite nights and if we have any needs.

When giving these gifts, be sincere. Call the office and ask to speak with the person in charge of receiving gifts. Some businesses must be careful about all gifts given; be sure to clarify that you want to offer a gift from your ministry. All they may need is reassurance that you expect nothing in return; you simply want to thank their staff or offer support/encouragement. When delivering gifts, reach out to your point-of-contact to make arrangements that are convenient for them.

These contacts serve a greater purpose than providing your church help; they are souls for whom our Savior died. These people need to be recognized and celebrated as individuals; their education and expertise when you need to 'phone-a-friend' are simply perks earned through relationship building. Celebrating the work of people who love on a community traditionally ignored in society is a worthy cause.

You are being the hands and feet of Jesus when you love on the community around you. This creates an opportunity to share with others what makes you different.

In 1 Corinthians 3:6-9 NIV we read:

I planted the seed, Apollos watered it, but God has been making it grow. So, neither the one who plants nor the one who waters is anything, but only God, who makes things grow. The one who plants and the one who waters have one purpose, and they will each be rewarded according to their own labor. For we are co-workers in God's service; you are God's field, God's building.

This begins a subject that we must address.

For some of the people with whom we work, we are simply meant to be planters in their lives; we will never see those seeds grow. Maybe we are waterers. Seeds have to be watered multiple times before growth can be seen with our eyes.

Our world is a spiritual desert. Some people are naturally cacti. Their faith comes easily to them, and they can withstand arid spiritual conditions with little to no water. Most people are not like this. Most need consistent watering. Now, to the point:

You may not see growth. This does not devalue what you do!

You may unintentionally encourage one of the people you bless to go back to church. But you may never know because their home denomination is different from yours. **That is a Kingdom win!**

You may encourage a person you bless to watch your services online and never know they are there. They are still hearing the word. They are still growing. **That is a Kingdom win!**

You may be planting a seed that will be watered ten years from now, in a city you've never visited, and there it may grow. **That is a Kingdom win!**

Not knowing is the hardest thing I have ever encountered in ministry. I do not operate well in maybes. I don't function well with missing information. This is a struggle for me. Maybe, just maybe, it's a struggle for you, too. Did God lay it on your heart? Do it anyway. Do it without proof. Do it without concrete evidence. Do it without the next step. Do it with faith that seeks no evidence. Faith is the confidence in what we hope for and assurance of what we do not see (Heb 11:1). Have faith. Do what God says. Because only God knows who is being reached. Only God knows how they are being changed. Only God knows why He said jump, but we have this promise:

- If I plant the seed and you water it;
- If I never get to see it grow and you do;
- If all I have is obedience;
- If all you have is a sprout before that seed blooms somewhere else, we both can take heart in this promise,

The one who plants and the one who waters have one purpose, and **they will each be rewarded according to their own labor**. For we are co-workers in God's service; you are God's field, God's building. (V. 8,9)

I am so thankful to co-labor with you. If you are reading this book, we may have some differing theology. Our churches may look different, sound different, or even worship different. But if you are reading this book, I have full confidence in this, you are a Christ-follower. You want to see people come to God. You want to see their lives changed by the love of a Savior. I am proud to co-labor for Christ with you, even if we never meet this side of Heaven.

The bottom line is this: whether it's you or me or Reverend Jimmy Bob in Nantucket, Tennessee, who gets to tell these people you impact why you were different, why you cared, they will hear it. They will hear and it will give them a chance to encounter the God who loves them – who loves us all. That chance worth it every time, and I know you agree with me.

Would you spend two hours and $30 to bring one person to Jesus? I would. No, we never know how many people these gifts will touch, but we do know that it will open doors. We do know that seeing the world from their view will make us better ministers. Of these things we can be sure.

I hope it doesn't seem like too much. I hope this doesn't feel overwhelming. It's not a one-person job; God will raise up volunteers to help you. He will send those who need you and your ministry. Before you can minister to them, there will be some hurdles to jump. There are some obstacles that come with special needs ministry, and we will address those next. It is more than doable with simple changes and just a hint of flexibility.

Jumping the Hurdles

Wonderful. Amazing. Chaotic. Inspirational.
Unexpected. Strange. Incredible. Impactful. Creative. Blessed.
Overwhelming. Loving. Rewarding. Fulfilling. Priceless.

These are some of the words I would use to describe working in ministry. I never would have imagined that I would be a pastor. But God doesn't call the qualified, He qualifies the called. Knowing that the people reading this have lived through the year 2020 in all of its glory, I know you understand exactly how crazy ministry can be. How it can change in the blink of an eye.

Here's something you may not know: many of your disabled brothers and sisters already had this skill. They have always had to be resourceful. Here is the thing about special needs ministry: you will become resourceful, too. You will. It's the nature of the blessing. I could never predict all the struggles you will face, but here's a few I am certain many of you will have:

- Church resistance
- Budgets
- Non-accessible buildings
- Finding and training volunteers
- Communication struggles
- Behavioral concerns

Yes, that list is a rather good start. We will tackle each of these struggles throughout this chapter. This is just an overview, but at the end of this book there will be contact information with which to reach me for further questions.

Church Resistance:

Almost every church has well-meaning people who love God. But people are flawed and broken. One of the side effects of brokenness is the dislike and fear of change. If you are reading this book, something has placed special needs ministry on your heart. Wonderful! The fact is, most churches have more than one person in leadership. I do not know where you are in the process of getting this ministry approved, so I am going to start at the very beginning. But first, a personal and completely applicable story.

In the winter of 2015, I sat on my deep freezer talking with a friend. I looked at her and shared a vision God placed on my heart of "...an accessible church." She was 100% for it because she was a special education teacher. Sitting there, in my pajamas on my freezer, God affirmed a calling on my life. My thing.

Our tiny church has four board members. At the time, one of them happened to be my father-in-law. Dad has always been numbers driven. A heart wrapped up in logic. I pitched the idea to him. I shared the two scriptures I have found that support special needs ministry (I was *so* not a pastor here, y'all). He looked at me, smiled, and said, "What about the liability?"

Now I know I have not shared much of my story with you, so here's a doozy. When I was growing up, my mother proudly declared herself a Wiccan and my father was a Jehovah's Witness. They met in a bar (insert joke here). Surprisingly, I was not raised in Christianity. No, I came to this faith when I met my husband and his family. We were 14 and he and his father shared the gospel with me. Yes, without that man who smiled down at me and said, "What about the liability?" I shudder to think who I would be.

Years of abuse sent my brain in a tailspin with that one statement. *This is never going to happen. What are you thinking? They are going to know you don't fit into the church. Just tell our lead pastor never mind. Don't do it!* Those words blared inside of my head. Yet there was a still, small voice. "I have called you to do this." I focused intently on that voice.

Searching for it, over the next two months as I prepared to speak to the board. Then the day came. There, I looked at my father-in-law, whom I was certain didn't approve, and this group of people, half of whom knew me unsaved and said, "Um...I think God is calling us to have a special needs ministry at this church. And...um...I think I was meant to lead it. Jenn is going to help, too."

To this day, that is still the most terrifying thing I have ever done for God.

I share to tell you I understand the anxiety. I know how it feels when you feel outnumbered and under-qualified. My best piece of advice is this: If God has called you to do this...do it. Find a way to do it. Maybe that means befriending a family with special needs members. Doing life with them and inviting them to church. Maybe it means a full-fledged ministry. Even if your church leaders seem resistant, that doesn't mean you cannot be Jesus to this area of the population. If you are met with disagreement on your calling, give them this book. Maybe they just need to see its being done elsewhere. But first, wrap everything you do in prayer.

Pray: Pray for the Holy Spirit to lead them. Not every church is prepared to grow in this way, but if you are called to it, God will place you somewhere the seed will grow. Where you are now may be that place, even if it doesn't seem like it. Abram waited 25 years. Nehemiah waited 4 months. They both *waited*. I pray patience over your waiting period and discernment so you may know if God is moving you.

It is imperative that if you are ever called to leave your church, ***don't*** leave with malice. Plenty of division in the church exists today without creating more. Pray. Cover everything you do in earnest prayer. Ask God to make clear the next steppingstone on the path you are meant to take.

Budgets:

This is a struggle for many churches. Even churches with large budgets have to be intentional about how they spend the funds they have. Our special needs ministry functions on a $1200 annual budget. Maybe yours can function on more. Maybe you don't have that much. Whatever you have, take heart: the love you share matters far more than the money you spend.

Here's the good news – assuming your church has a printer, you can start a special needs ministry for under $100. Yes, I am serious. You can get the bare minimum things you need to kick-start this ministry for under $100. There are two rules to special needs ministry on a budget. First, second hand in good shape is good stewardship. Second, limit patterns and color variety.

Here's a must-have list:

- Quiet space
- Noise canceling headphones: $15
- Fidgets: Multipack $20, Playdough $2, Rice and other sensory items $10
- Basic art supplies (markers, crayons, coloring books)
- 10lb weighted blanket: $40
- Communication cards: $4 + lanyard $2 (or make your own for free!) Here are some cards you will want to be sure are included:
    1. All done
    2. Stop
    3. Drink

4. Hungry
5. Wait
6. Listen
7. Break please
8. More
9. Quiet
10. No touching/nice hands
11. Yes
12. No

Bonus points if you add conversational options to the lanyard so your buddies can communicate with those around them.

This list is not comprehensive. Over time, we have gathered more things. Here is a list of the things our ministry has gathered over the years:

- 7-foot bean bag chair we got on sale: $150
- Foam blocks: $5 from a secondhand store
- Books, variety: dollar store
- Crash pad: donated
- Foldable foam chairs: donated
- Pod swing: $35
- More fidgets (heads up, you will probably always need more fidgets)
- Carpet squares

As you can see, starting your ministry can be done very affordably with moderate outreach. We do everything we do with a $1200 budget every year. Here's the great news: there are a ton of thing you can do at little to no cost. Here is my go-to list:

- Story Hour: Borrow a book from your nursery (or your home), pick a date, grab some pretzels (optional) and read a great book to some great kids. Want to go all out? Create a corresponding craft. These don't have to be expensive and should be something relatively anyone could do with a little help. See the back of the book for my go to crafts. Event cost? $10.

○ Movie Night: Everyone loves the movies! Have your buddies bring their families and some pillows for movie night. Make popcorn and offer water. Pick a movie, and make sure your quiet place is available. You will want two volunteers in the quiet area and yourself and some youth volunteers (or adults) in the movie room. Event cost: $15 with movie rental.

○ Volunteering at Special Olympics or a Night to Shine: ABSOLUTELY FREE.

○ Craft hours: Create clothes pin butterflies or paint some rocks, just have fun. Cost: $10-20

○ Worship Night: A chance for some of your buddies to worship in a quieter setting. I would encourage having two different events twice a year. One night that is sensory safe (quiet) and one that is set up for them to make the music. Pro hack: Use a craft night to create your own instruments with things that most would throw away: coffee can drums, toilet paper shakers, empty bottle maracas. The options are basically endless. $0 unless you purchase toy instruments.

The goal of these events is to be as accessible as possible, but what to do if your church isn't disability accessible?

Building Blues

Not all buildings are created equal in the ministry world. This should come as no shock to anyone. Issues like storage, ministry space, and accessibility are common. For obvious reasons, the most impactful issue in special needs ministry is that not all churches are disability accessible. If the building was built before the 1960s, it is probably not. I know our building is not disability friendly. To an extent, if you don't have a $500,000 budget to make your church ADA accessible, you do what you can.

Unfortunately, unless we meet face to face and I walk through your church, I cannot see all the issues you may face. As able-bodied individuals, it's often hard to grasp the struggles our brothers and sisters with different abilities may face. It may also make it harder for us to predict what will cause issues for those with sensory acuity problems. However, I have included a list for you of things that may be worth considering.

1. **Stairs**

   Stairs pose significant difficulty for those with physical disabilities. It's easy to see the struggle for our wheelchair bound brothers and sisters, of course! Stairs can effectively make it impossible for them to join in areas where there are stairs but no elevator or ramps. But physical disabilities have varying degrees, just like mental disabilities. Some people may be able to use stairs, but they may be at greater risk of falls due to low muscle tone or other unseen struggles. Make sure that all stairs in your building have at least one secure handrail. Have someone walk with the individual for additional safety.

How do we deal with this issue? Short of putting in an elevator, it requires creativity and some intentional thought. Place ramps wherever possible. Ramps help create accessible areas. When possible, meet on the ground floor to assure that everyone can be involved. Speak to those in your congregation who are physically disabled or wheelchair bound. They will be able to tell you what would help them the most and will feel important because you asked. The elderly can also provide a great deal of wisdom as they often face physical impactions.

2. **Doorways**

   It is easy to overlook things like the width of a doorway, but the fact is most wheelchairs require a doorway that is at least 32 inches wide. If your doorways are narrower than this, it can prevent a wheelchair user from independently accessing that area.

   One of my favorite creative techniques is to have an extra wheelchair in the room and just transfer the individual from one to the other as needed. (This option is not feasible in our building: our bathroom doorways are narrow, and there is another wall near the entry that creates an impossible turn radius for chairs.)

   Short of extensive renovation, there is little that can be done about narrow doorways. Do your best; people *will* be able to tell.

   Make sure all your bathrooms are equipped with handrails to assist in standing as well. This is a very affordable adaption that goes a long way in helping those with physical disabilities maintain independence.

3. **Counter Heights**

   There are many disabilities out there that affect height, but the most prevalent is probably dwarfism. There are many types of dwarfism, and the mobility very much depends on the individual situation. The great thing is that these adaptions are relatively easy.

   Make sure every bathroom is equipped with a step stool (preferably with a handle for safety) and a grabbing tool if things like spare toilet paper or paper towels are stored above four feet high.

4. **Sensory Safe Colors**

   This is an extremely easy win that almost any church could enact. For many people with disabilities, bright colors and busy rooms become overwhelming. This can lead to behaviors such as aggression, inability to focus, and meltdowns. I strongly suggest a neutral color scheme for paint in common and sensory friendly areas. You can use decorations to add color if you wish. These are easy to remove in case a guest becomes overwhelmed. This will benefit your neurotypical children as well. All children are prone to being overwhelmed and distracted. The good news is this is as simple a fix as a paint job!

5. **Room**

   Not every church has a plethora of rooms. I know our church does not. We count ourselves blessed to have a dedicated sensory safe area. This is not the case for everyone. There are a lot of areas that are great to have when you work with adults and children with disabilities. Spaces like a sensory safe room, adult accessible changing station, and multiple classrooms are nice. Having the room for them is another issue. So, what do you do?

To a certain extent, many rooms can share multiple functions. For example, the location we change teens and adults who are incontinent is the same location we would change a child. Make sure the room offers privacy. I would strongly encourage you, especially when changing a teen or adult, to have two adults present.

We enact this at every age in our ministry. All the brokenness in our world spotlights the beauty of being above reproach for all.

A sensory safe area could potentially be shared with a cry room. Simply post a sign that says something like this:

> *We love your babies,*
> *And we love you,*
> *But our disabled friends need this room, too.*
> *Thanks in advance for your willingness to share,*
> *So all can connect with God here.*

What can I say, I enjoy writing a little poem every once in a while.

If you absolutely do not have space for a devoted sensory safe room, I understand. Create sensory bags mentioned earlier in this book. Find a quiet place you can take the child to calm down, even if it is a hallway. Go for a walk if the child is safe. Do what you can with what is available to you in your building, and do more when and if you can. For most families with impacted children, you are trying will speak loud enough that you will never need to shout we love you!

Finding and training volunteers

It's the age-old question all churches ask -- where am I going to get the volunteers? The good news is, you probably already have them. If not, look to people in your community with a heart for those with disabilities who would be willing to jump in and help. Here is the basic list of things to know about seeking volunteers:

1. Not every buddy will need a 1:1 volunteer.
2. Teens make fantastic children's volunteers.
3. Inclusion is the way to go! It minimizes your need for volunteers and maximizes learning for all involved.
4. You can reach out to your community for volunteers.

Sometimes, volunteers need to fill multiple roles. They may serve on Sunday morning to keep a buddy safe and help absorb as much as possible from a lesson. They may be needed on a respite night to assist with cooking a meal. They may be needed to care for a buddy while the parents seek counsel. The list goes on.

Here's the great thing, if you have a children's ministry, you already have many of these facets in place. Much of disability ministry can be grown out of a children's ministry because the goals are similar: to provide the person a safe place to grow; to provide a chance for the parent to worship peacefully; most important, this ministry offers the chance to deepen the individual's personal relationship with God.

You are probably doing this in some capacity at present; now we take those goals and apply them to the disabled in your church. By extension, you can apply them to the disabled in your community. The point here is that you have volunteers who are 75% of the way there.

However, much can be done with limited volunteers. Create 'Buddy Bags' so those with disabilities can have access to helpful coping tools. Hold a small group for adults and teens with disabilities. Have a parent's luncheon and share a devotional. Once relationships are established, have one member from the church visit families to encourage and disciple each member as individuals.

Begin with love, the people who benefit most from these ministries will also become its champions as they mature in their faith.

Communication

A large number of those impacted by disabilities have communication struggles. They may be hard of hearing or deaf, or they may respond to visual communication cues. We must take time to reconsider how we 'do' church and discipleship. But change and growth are good things.

Sign language is not always easy to learn, but almost anyone can learn some. I strongly encourage people to learn ASL and become as fluent as possible. Personally, doing much more than the basics has been an uphill journey because I have fine motor difficulties. So I understand the challenges people may have; consistent effort is imperative.

For basic communication ability with both the deaf community and those with developmental or language delays, I recommend learning a few words in ASL:

- Yes
- No
- Wait
- Bathroom/toilet
- All done

- Hurt
- Hungry
- Thirsty
- Stop
- More

If you or your buddy does not know sign language, many other methods of communication can be used instead. For example, place several pictures on a key ring of places or items a buddy may need to utilize. A bathroom door, noise canceling headphones, a water bottle, and other common images can be used as means of communication. In a pinch, it never hurts to ask yes or no questions and assign each answer to one of your hands.

Communication is crucial. If you are intentional, you can find a way to communicate. Fortunately, only a small percentage of communication is actually expressed verbally. Most intention and meaning is sent and received through vocal inflection, facial expression, and body language. I encourage you to remember you *can* communicate with those who are non-verbal. *Being unable to speak doesn't mean that a person has nothing to say. We just have to learn to listen differently.*

Behavior

I put these back-to-back intentionally because we must recognize that behavior *is* communication. Every behavior has a need behind it. Like detectives, sometimes we must search to find it. In general, we have little time to self-evaluate and identify our needs. Because of this, our coping mechanisms and natural responses to stress are sometimes unhealthy and unproductive. People with disabilities have a similar plight for a different reason: they don't know *how* to evaluate, decide, and express what they may need.

I have seen varying types of behaviors in this field. I have been bitten, peed on, hit, cursed at, and threatened. **But,** I have also been high-fived, hugged, and kissed (let's be honest, that one can be a little uncomfortable in a professional realm.) I have worked in this field for ten years (six in ministry), I am a mother to two disabled children, and I am the big sister to a beautiful young woman who is developmentally two years old. After sharing my education and experience, I confidently tell you this: people who have extreme behaviors have them because they have extreme unmet needs.

I am not suggesting abuse or neglect. I am instead stating that most behavior, in my opinion, is a reaction to our body's natural fight, flight, or freeze response. Creating a coping plan is imperative, but it cannot be done alone. As a church, you must work with the parents to decided when redirecting will be enough, when a parent should be called and under what circumstances it is appropriate to take hold of a child. Each family and child will be different. Here is an example though:

Tommy is a sweet 8-year-old boy with Down syndrome. Tommy is a light, almost always laughing and smiling. Today when he walks into children's church, Tommy seems a little off. He does well for the first 15 minutes or so, but after the music ends, Tommy begins to scream and hit himself. He clearly is not ready for the music to stop and has become agitated, but class must continue.

As the teacher continues, you are the one responsible for assuring Tommy's safety, as well as helping to re-establish an environment where Tommy's peers can learn. Tommy doesn't currently have a plan of action for behaviors like this. There are several choices you can make:

1. You can call Tommy's parents and have them come to the children's area to help calm him.

2. You can redirect Tommy and see if that works, focusing his attention elsewhere.
3. You can hold Tommy's arms to prevent him from hurting himself.
4. You can carry Tommy to the sensory safe room.

Let me let you in on a little secret, in this situation there is one best answer. Because no plan is in place, you must call Tommy's parents for help. They can teach you what works best for Tommy and help redirect his frustration. You cannot safely do any of the other options without a plan to know effectively how to help. Tommy's parents must be called to make the final decision.

I do want to address number three. When a child self-injuring, our natural response is to make it stop, to force them to stop hitting themselves. Many places offer classes on safe restraint, but significant mental implications to the child exist when the restraining person is untrained. In this situation, you would want the parents to be the main voice on the decision-making team. As ministry volunteers or pastors, we are not to tell them what has to be done, we are to love their children and show Christ to their entire family.

In our ministry, the standard of care is this: we will protect other children by removing them if a situation becomes volatile. We will protect the child by offering valid and safe options for calming down. We will only use restraint (like grabbing, lifting, and holding against a child's will) in a critical safety situation (the child is injuring another child, running out in the street, or seriously self-injuring.) When restraint is used it will be done for as little time possible. We do this for a few reasons:

◇ Trust – we want the child to be able to trust us.

- Safety – of volunteers as well as the child, a child being restrained is more likely to cause a severe injury to themselves.
- There are other, better, more effective ways of dealing with behavior than grabbing the child.

So what are those ways?

Start with a plan. When you welcome a new person with a disability into your church, make sure to speak to the caregiver about basics. What techniques calm them? How can they safely be taken to a calm-down area? When should you call the parents? What triggers responses like Tommy had? Perhaps Tommy just needed a warning the music was going away. Having not been told the schedule could have exacerbated the issue.

In his situation, here is what I would have done: I would have spoken to Tommy in a calm, level voice and asked, "Tommy, are you upset because we turned off the music – yes, or no?"

If Tommy answered, I would then evaluate what to do next – if yes, offer him a place to continue listening to music for a few extra minutes – and if no, I would ask him, "Can we go take a break for a few minutes? We can go play in our special calm room until we are ready to come back and join class."

Maybe this would work, maybe it would not, but if neither of these things worked, I would then send someone to get his parents. I would reassure them no one is upset with Tommy, we just want to help him.

Without a plan, if a buddy's behavior cannot be deescalated via redirection or a break, the parent must always be called. If there is a plan in place that says I can pick up

Tommy and carry him to the sensory safe room, I can do that. Plans are vital. They serve a dual purpose: they alleviate liability and ensure parents, caregivers, and buddies all feel heard and safe in the church. As such, let me include an example of one of the behavioral plans we currently have in our church (names have been changed.)

Buddy Behavior Plan

Behavior is communication—listen to what the person is saying.

Buddy Name: Jack B   **Date of Birth:** 1/26/__

Duration of intervention: 1 year   **Date:** 8/17/2021

Primary Diagnosis: Autism Spectrum Disorder (comorbid emotional regulation disorder).

Goals:

1. Reintegrate into church setting.
2. Voice needs clearly without physical violence.
3. Create and sustain friendships with peers.

Replacement behaviors:

1. Redirection: Help Jack focus on something else (fidget, music, deep breaths).
2. Removal (take him to the sensory safe room).
3. Request - if Jack doesn't calm down within 15 minutes in the sensory safe room contact his mother.

Behavior Plan:

If Jack becomes violent then one embrace volunteer will interact with him. They will keep talking to a minimum and will not physically touch Jack unless it is a situation of imminent harm. Non-violent intervention if necessary to keep Jack from imminent harm. Buddy may block hits and kicks with arms but is not permitted to grab or push away Jack. He will calm down shortly after outburst and need reassurance you still care about him and that you do not hate him. Please provide this support. If outburst lasts longer than 10 minutes, send someone to get Jack's mother Amy from service. If outburst has occurred inform Amy after service.

Top three pointers for working through the challenges of working with special needs individuals:

1. Preparation. Having a plan is everything. When you welcome a new child or adult with disabilities into your church, always speak to the caregiver. Ask them what their child likes, what they are good at, and what triggers meltdowns or other behaviors. Ask them for calming techniques that work at home. Also be sure to ask if a problem occurs, how quickly do they want to be contacted. Make sure there is a safe, quiet space available, and have a buddy bag they can take along. These steps will lessen the probability of a significant issue.

2. Autonomy. Just like everyone else, persons with special needs must have bodily autonomy. They have the right to say no to touch. This right is only able to be infringed upon when there is a case of imminent harm (a presumable risk of severe harm coming to the child/adult.)

3. Connection. To minimize the risk of challenging behaviors or events, you *must* get to know your people. Create a safe place that can be easily secured (prevent eloping, running into dangerous traffic), have a volunteer buddy available in case of a problem, and have a schedule that is visually accessible. With these provisions in place, there is less likely to be a severe situation.

Now, if I have not scared you away, there is no doubt a question on your mind. "If we are to welcome people with disabilities into our church, how do we support their spiritual needs?" The next chapter is designed to help you take those first steps.

Pastoring the Disabled

So, where does one even begin? This is a community that has been burned by the lack of compassion in the church, so how do we begin to repair the damage? Maybe you don't agree that the church has had a lack of compassion, and I understand why you would think that. We only know that which we experience, which is a normal side effect of the shortsightedness in humanity.

I explain it to my kids like this. We see in 2-D, and God sees in 3-D. He sees more of the details in the picture than we do, but we are both looking at the same picture.

I recognize that I know little of what it means to be a black woman because I am not black. That doesn't mean that I don't care about people of other races, it just means this is not my unique experience. I may not effectively show compassion unless I can find a point of connection. As such, I listen to the stories of my brothers and sisters of color, validate their feelings, and find common ground. From here, we can move forward and forge a friendship because we have common ground.

No one can ask us to know what it is to be everyone. As Christians, we are responsible for caring about and including everyone. We are to make sure to leave space at the table for everyone. Much like racism has been (and dare I say, remains to be) a problem in the church, so does ableism.

I use the word "remains" intentionally. God always provided for the support, care, and value of the disabled into His plan. There was always a place for society's relegated members. What we are talking about here, friends, is a change of narrative. A recognition that we do not see the whole picture. For that reason, maybe someone has a different view. The fact that you are reading this book tells me you recognize the disparity here. Well done! Once we recognize that and see the harsh treatment the disabled and their families experience, we can address them as people with unique experiences. Please don't tune me out yet—what is next is far too valuable to ignore.

The disabled community is one of the most notoriously overlooked on the invite list. As a whole, the church has lacked compassion because it has subconsciously lacked the intentionality to identify the similarities and reconcile the differences to ensure inclusion remains a fabric of our faith. We can change this, and with the help of the Holy Spirit we can see people as God does.

Dignity for All

"I don't want to be like everyone else, I just want to be treated like I matter as much as everyone else." – Jairmie

My son is 10 years old. Recently, he came home from school and realized for the very first time what different really means. He was in class, and they were taking turns reading. When it was his turn, class was almost over and the teacher decided to let his para read for him because she would be faster. In that moment, Jairmie realized that – while in our family different is not bad – to the world it means you matter less. It means his voice matters less. This wrecked him. He lost a lot of dignity and we spent the entire week trying to rebuild him. We are not even half way to that goal. The quote above is from the day he came home broken and in tears.

These last two pandemic affected school years have depleted teachers, and I understand that. We did have a conversation about it, but it was laced with much grace. She is tired, overworked, and overwhelmed. Jairmie is so happy-go-lucky, she never imagined he would be hurt.

I share this story to let you know two things:

1. You are not trained in this field; mistakes will happen, and most will forgive you if your approach them with humility.
2. The one thing I told my boy that has clicked, that has worked, is this: "We don't compare ourselves to others because God did not make us in their image, He made us in His." The church would be better if we would recognize that all people are image bearers. We are all equal at the foot of the cross, and God has bestowed dignity upon us that the church should do nothing but affirm.

Each and every person has God-given worth. One of the pieces of advice most often given to those working with the disabled population is this: presume competence. Talk to people in an age-appropriate way. Watch for them to communicate their needs. Talk to the person, not about them. Let them have a voice in what they are doing. Allow them a safe place to process emotion. Stop trying to recreate people into the image society wants them to be; start empowering them to become that who God made them to be. Everyone deserves dignity and autonomy, even if they cannot say it out loud.

Important Vocabulary

One of the most colorful things in ministry is the people we work with, am I right? Well, the model of ministry I execute best is to do life with people; as such, many of the people I work with, my children meet as well. Combine that with the lack of filter their autism gives them, and please give me grace. Years ago, my children repeated others like a two-year-old does, with confidence and not a care in the world.

My son Kaiden had a teacher who didn't enjoy teaching him. He is my spunkier child and much harder to get to submit when you want him to. We were at a parent-teacher conference, and the exacerbated teacher made a flippant comment, "I didn't sign up to work with retards like your son, so I don't really know what you want me to tell you."

I was taken aback by her words. I know she is a general education teacher, but that was a little...shall I say, abrasive. I was rendered temporarily speechless, which is not a condition I experience often, but in my silence my son said one of those colorful words the boys were exposed to by the people I work with. Without skipping a beat or looking away from his fidget, my kindergarten child says, "You're a dumbass."

Look, the minister in me was mortified, but the mama in me was not. This was true for two reasons. First, it was an appropriate place in the conversation to interject that he was not pleased with what she said. Second, it was spot on. Her statement demonstrated ignorance.

I share this story to bring up an obvious point: our words matter. The way we talk to, and about people matters, even if we think they are not listening. I am certain his teacher didn't think he was paying attention. But he was. Your buddies will be listening, too. Be intentional about what you say.

'Person-first' language versus 'identity-first' language.

For most disabilities it's important to recognize the person first. Becky has cerebral palsy versus the cripple Becky. It is pretty rude to call Becky a cripple. There are some words and phrases that are much greyer, though. Even if you don't know much about disability, you probably do know there is a thriving deaf community. The have their own culture.

The same can be said of the Autistic community. There are many persons with autism who prefer what they call 'identity-first' language. There are many reasons for this, and I want to respect your time, so I am going to give you the best advice I can. Listen to how the disabled talk about their disability. Listen to how their caregivers speak. Do they 'have autism' or are they 'autistic'?

Ask questions. Listen when someone says something is offensive. Apologize if you offend someone. It will be easy to get the hang of over time. I have a friend who has a daughter with down syndrome. She calls her daughter her 'little Downie.' What may be a term of endearment for the mother/daughter relationship is not going to be for someone else, so I would never use that term. The goal is to recognize the inherent, God-given value of those with disabilities and affirm it with our words.

Supporting Your Buddies

Each buddy you care for will have different needs. I cannot give you a recipe for supporting all people, but I can tell you this, people with disabilities have the same needs as everyone else. Food, water, shelter, love, recognition, friendship, a real relationship with God, and any other need we have on a daily basis.

One of the greatest gifts we can give our buddies is to support them in seeking to fulfill these needs. We need to encourage kids to include them to the best of their abilities. We need to make sure we are cheering them on. We need to show them a love that is unbreakable by their behaviors. We need to take care of their physical needs.

Sometimes this means feeding them because they cannot feed themselves; sometimes it means ensuring the safety of a child who tries to leave the building unsupervised. For others, this means changing their diapers. I know, no one wants to talk about that, but can you imagine sitting in a soiled diaper for an entire church service?

Supporting the needs of these buddies is much simpler when we ask ourselves, "What do I need, and of those needs what may this buddy need at this time?"

In the back of this book, there is an example of the spiritual IEP's I wrote to assist those who wish to benefit from spiritual growth. These are designed for both those with disabilities, as well as neurotypical individuals who want a more intentional approach of growing their faith and having a more real relationship with God.

We have talked about behavioral struggles previously, but there are many other great resources available for details on how to handle such struggles. I strongly encourage you to check out KeyMinistry.org and follow their blogs. Signing up is free and there is much to be learned. Here is an example on behavior:

> The one contributing factor to aggressive behavior you can influence as a ministry leader is the environment in which your kids worship, learn, and serve at church. You want to consider how you can create environments that help all kids to maximize their capacity to use all of their cognitive resources for the best possible experience at church. – Steven Grcevich, M.D.

When Kids Become Aggressive at Church — Key Ministry

I encourage you to read the entire article and check out more on special needs ministry in general. You will even find some of my own writing on Keyministry.com.

With a little bit of research and planning, you can enable children of all abilities to be successful in your church. It will take some trial and error but with the parents on your team, you will not fail if you don't give up on them.

Supporting Parents of Impacted Children

As a special-needs mama myself, there are some days that I just feel so alone. Few people understand the pressure that lies ahead of me. Will my children be independent? Will they marry? Do they understand the things I am teaching them? Am I failing somehow? When do I cross over the point from being an advocate to being a bully (yes, that is really a thing!)?

I don't know what it is like to be a parent of neurotypical children. I talk to them, but there is a disconnect. We share some of the same struggles, but so many others are so different.

Supporting families with disabled children is a simple idea, but enacting it can be a little more complex. Here are some basic ideas:

Create a space that is safe for parents and caregivers to be open and honest about their feelings. We do this through a monthly breakfast. I've heard others who do it by hosting a small group. It's really whatever you feel comfortable with, as long as it is private, safe, and has food. Okay – the last one isn't necessary, but who doesn't like free food!

Create a culture of openness in the church. Share your struggles. Be honest! And yes, I mean from the pulpit. Let others share their stories as well. Let other share how God turned trials into triumphs and terror into thankfulness.

Check on them. We all need to matter. Create a schedule and reach out weekly and monthly.

Provide a chance to find rest. A retreat. A respite night. A coffee break. Encourage someone in the church make them dinner. It's not your place to do everything; as pastors, we *are* called to empower the body to serve. Maybe you can schedule one person in the church to be a monthly respite provider for another church family. Maybe you will do a respite night. The options are limitless.

Provide for eventual practical needs. For parents whose children have medically complex issues, sometimes things come up. The church can be the hands and feet by providing for the physical needs of a family if that is within the budget.

Help special needs families get connected. We were meant to do life together. We need each other. Typically, special needs families retreat into themselves. Helping them connect with other families will lessen the isolation and the mental load.

Ask them what they need – and keep asking. We have all been there. Someone asks us if we need anything and we reply with, "No, I'm fine," when we are really not fine at all. So, care enough to ask consistently. Do you need prayer for anything? How are your kids doing? How are you doing? Do you need anything? Hey, I was thinking of you today. Let me know if there is anything you need. A little love goes a long way.

The Non-diagnosed Impacted

Not everyone with a disability has a diagnosis. Not everyone with a diagnosis speaks openly about their disability. The word disability has multiple definitions. One of these, according to dictionary.com, is: (3) anything that disables or puts one at a disadvantage.

I am here to tell you this – there are people in your congregation with undiagnosed physical, mental, neurological and developmental disabilities. If they don't seem to be learning the way you teach, or they don't seem to be growing the way others are, there's a good chance you are dealing with a different neurotype or a possible disability. Have grace. Be patient. Try new ways of teaching and interacting. These people are needed members of the body of Christ, too. *Point of clarification: do not tell them to go see a doctor and find out what is wrong with them!* Adapt yourself and your teaching style to be more inclusive.

Developing a Culture of Inclusion

Think of the church as a tapestry, beautifully woven with all the colors of the rainbow. Now remove the yellow. Does that tapestry have the same effect? Of course not.

We must weave people of all abilities into our church. For we are all God's workmanship. Like the Bible describes us as a body – each part equally important – if we are to successfully welcome the disabled into our churches, we must see their value. There are so many pieces of advice I could give you, but your time is valuable so let's settle on the top two.

1. *Be a voice to those without one.*

There are people with bad theology in your church. There are people with good intentions that make Jesus look like a bad guy. There are people whose faith in God is so huge it will stumble a little one in Christ. We are all human, and at times this means that we will inevitably hurt people. As leaders, we must work to correct erroneous theology. We must work to portray an accurate image of Christ, and we must educate people before they become stumbling blocks.

We start by teaching an accurate view of God – recognizing Him as a healer as well as the God who told so many in the Bible no.

We start by openly discussing disabilities and mental illness from the pulpit, and in our own day to day conversations. We make it clear to our churches that everyone is welcome here, and we follow up in our words and actions.

And, when necessary, we start by admonishing in love those who are not correctly representing Christ.

2. *Celebrate differences.*

This one seems really simple; in its purest form, it is very simple. God created each of us differently. We each have different strengths and weaknesses. It's beautiful when you think about it. He created us to need each other. To need our community. Much like the triune God himself.

We must create a culture that celebrates the differences as strengths, not weaknesses. As a church, we should be open to those who look, sound, and learn differently, and even those who share different ideals. We should long for everyone to find hope in Christ.

This is the very basics because the fact is each church will look different. There are so many people who would love to consult on a case-by-case basis. You can see some of them in the back of the book. These two steps will take time to implement correctly. Why? Because deep changes happen slowly. The Grand Canyon was formed by water wearing down the rock, but it wasn't formed overnight. These changes will be slow but consistent if you are intentional about implementing the suggestions above. Even better – your church will be healthier because of it.

Empowering the Disabled to Serve

We mentioned this briefly earlier and I just want to touch on this one more time in a little more detail. We empower the disabled to serve by creating environments in which they can effectively share their giftings. This is how we empower anyone to serve.

Every disabled person has different support needs, just like every able-bodied person. Here are some things that may help to further support children and adults with special needs in their desire to serve.

- A check list
- A visual schedule
- A timer
- Noise canceling headphones
- A clear routine
- A buddy to serve with them

Creating a place for the disabled to serve.

We have drilled in this point – we all have a purpose that was ordained by God. A good work we are made to do. These gifting do not somehow miss the disabled and the mentally ill. No, your disabled brothers and sisters have gifts of wisdom (that will sometimes come out of nowhere), knowledge (impeccable memories), prophecy (words from the Lord), worship (uninhibited, unrestrained worship of God), and all the other gifts God bestows upon His church. They can and must be used for the edification of the church.

So how do we do this?

We get to know them and see where they fit in. We allow them trial and error. We listen to them and observe their strengths. Then we encourage, teach, and deploy them to use the gift God has given them. Let me give you some examples:

- We have a young man who – when he is well enough – folds bulletins every Saturday night.
- We have a young woman who has greeted at our respite nights.
- We have a child who has taught adults what it means to worship, brought to tears of joy at the sound to worship music.
- We have a man with severe mental illness who speaks in tongues and translates.
- We have a pastor with mental, physical, and developmental disabilities.

We go deeper than just caring about their gifts in the church, we empower them to find a place they can serve in the community (food pantry, homeless shelter) as well as help support life and job skills as much as we can with each individual.

Because we do all these things, we have a stronger body of believers for it. As leaders in ministry, one of our chief goals must be equipping the saints to serve. This is something that you can do, friends. You *can* do this. This is not rocket science or incredibly complicated work. Walk in love. Value others above yourself. Impart dignity. Celebrate uniqueness. God is so faithful. He will give you exactly the wisdom and the grace you need. Trust Him – and jump.

Closing Words

How else could I start this? Thank you. Thank you for caring. Thank you for reading this. Thank you for noticing those who so often go unnoticed. Thank you.

I have included for you a list of over 30 images you can use for communication. I have included some crafts and sensory solutions that we use in our church to create a sensory friendly environment. The most important thing I have included here is my prayers for you all.

Even if you just take small steps towards inclusion, I know you will be taking huge leaps toward the heart of God. I pray He blesses you. Oh, I pray He blesses your whole church for your faithfulness.

I hope you have begun to realize how much we need each other. We need our disabled brothers and sisters as much as they need us. You can be a part of the solution. You can be missionaries to a population right next door that no one notices. I know you can do this because the very God who created you said, "Greater things will you do in my name than I have done." Sure we can heal the sick and cast out demons, but I encourage you to open your eyes to one other thing that Jesus did that we as a church must begin doing if we want to see a revival. What is that?

We must live in revolutionary love.

We must bind up the brokenhearted. We must set the captives free. We must bear one another's burdens. We must empower the saints and go into the world, storming the gates of Hell for all the souls who would come—and that includes the least of these. May God bless you.

Pastor Joanna French

Helpful Hacks

Sensory Musts:

Rice buckets: Include scoops or hide toys in them.

Water Beads

Shaving cream/whipped cream and food coloring: This provides a fantastic and messy experience. Of course, consider developmental age and allergies when deciding if you will use shaving or whipped cream.

Sensory bottles:

You will need an empty water bottle, clear glue, glitter, water, and super glue.

Add glue to the water bottle until half full.

Fill the rest of the bottle with water until one inch below the rim.

Add glitter of your choice.

Super glue the lid to the bottle (be careful, you don't want to glue yourself to it, too.)

Shake.

Bonus: Attach a tag that says do not drink on one side with a no drink on the other (See visual symbols.)

Respite Activities:

Crafts:

Clothes pin airplanes:

You will need clothes pins, tongue depressors, and paint.

The final product will look like this:

Tissue paper butterflies:

You will need: Clothes pins, pipe cleaners, and various colors of tissue paper.

The final product will look like this:

Toilet paper roll binoculars:

You will need: Two toilet paper rolls per student, clothes pins, glue, construction paper, twine, and a hole punch (to be operated by volunteer):

Allow your buddies to decorate their toilet paper rolls. Glue the two rolls together, then clamp with clothes pins. Allow to dry. Hole punch the outside edge of each binocular and tie twine to create a necklace.

Gumdrop tower:

You will need: Several bags of gum drops and plastic toothpicks (this avoids splinters.)

The final product will look like this:

Additional ideas:

Painted rocks

Suncatchers

Create a silly mask

Games

Balloon volleyball

You will need: A bag of balloons and a string to tie from one side of the room to the other. For added flare, add pool noodles to make the string easier to see. Don't take score. This is all about fun!

Bean bag toss

You will need: Baskets of varying sizes to attach different point values to (bigger basket = fewer points), bean bags, and painter's tape.

Set up the baskets, put down different pieces of tape for varying difficulties, and place the bean bag by the tape. Enjoy!

Pool noodle soccer:

You will need: Pool noodles and a thin piece of wood (plywood thickness.)

Curve pool noodle and securely tape it to the thin piece of wood. Then secure them to the ground with tape as well. Make sure this is tape that can be used on carpet if necessary. Final product will look like this:

Additional ideas:

Other super fun options include: Pillowcase sack races, cup stacking, and bowling.

Affordable Volunteer Appreciation Gift Ideas:

Buy an affordable puzzle (check your local dollar store) and attach a note that says, "We have the best team, and you are an important piece. Thank you!"

Purchase Almond Joy candy and add a note: "You bring joy to so many. Thank you!"

Buy individual chip bags and add a note: "You're all that and a bag of chips. Thank you!"

Purchase popcorn and add a note: "You make our team pop! Thank you for all you do!" This also works with soda.

Purchase mint flavored gum and attach a note that says, "This is "mint" to say thank you!"

Purchase a container of hand soap and attach a note saying, "Thanks for helping out with all the sticky situations!"

Purchase a small bundle of pencils (look during school season) and attach a note, "You are the 'write' person for the job. Thanks for all you do."

Purchase a coffee cup and add a note: "Thanks a latte' for all you do."

Buy a pair of comfy socks and add the note, "Socks off to you for being amazing!"

Buy a bag of life savers and add a note: "You are a real life saver."

Create a jar of M&Ms and label it 'Chill Pills' to give your volunteers a laugh.

Other ideas:

Host a volunteer appreciation dinner.

Host a game night for volunteers.

Spiritual Growth Plan:

Student's Name: Today's Date:

Student Profile

My student's learning style is:

My student's strengths:

Incentives that work for my student (what drives your student):

Things that do not support my student's growth (what doesn't work):

Limitations my student faces (I.E. short attention span, reading deficits, etc.):

What does my student like/dislike doing? How can I incorporate this spiritually?

Example:

George is seven years old. He knows one scripture by memory, John 3:16. George struggles in reading, but he enjoys art. He is an auditory learner, but he struggles to sit still. At church, he loves to sing worship music and sometimes even asks if he can have a microphone. He knows that prayer is talking to God. When you ask him to pray, he simply says, "Hey, God. It's George. Amen." During down time, George tends to tease other kids his age, but he is always willing to help new mothers in church by holding their little ones while they take a brief break. George is funny, loud, and unsure of himself. George responds well to being taught in a more individualized setting, in groups of no more than four at a time. He giggles when you ask him what the Holy Spirit is. When further prompted, he tells you that ghosts are pretend.

What are George's strengths?

What are George's possible next steps?

Where can George serve? What are the limitations on the service he can do?

What would be the best way to support George's spiritual growth outside of the church?

Example Goals:

Goal #1: George will learn two more memory verses: Proverbs 11:17 and I Corinthians 13:4. Once each scripture is memorized, George will get to go out with his parents for ice cream.

Goal #2: George will teach his little brothers the words to his favorite worship song: *I'm In the Lord's Army*. He will have a chance to serve by worshiping with them every day.

Goal #3: George will pray with his parents daily. He will learn to (1) ask, (2) praise, and (3) give thanks. We have broken prayer down into three steps because George struggles with more complicated instructions or lists.

Goal #4: George will be introduced to the Holy Spirit's role in the Trinity and the relationship of the Father and Jesus to the Holy Spirit. George will be told frequently that his love of babies may be one way God can use him to serve others in the church, and this may encourage him to find new ways to serve. "George, because you love the babies so much, can you help me wipe down the nursery after service today? We want to keep the babies safe by keeping the nursery clean."

Goal #5: George will take steps to become kinder to those of his age group. Those who are involved with George's spiritual growth plan will know to reference the above scriptures as reminders to be kind.

George has so much potential! Having a plan will help us see his growth, and it will help us hold ourselves accountable to encourage George to become the man God wants him to be.

Areas of growth:

Scripture:

These commandments that I give you today are to be on your hearts. Impress them on your children. Talk about them when you sit at home and when you walk along the road, when you lie down and when you get up.

Deuteronomy 6:6-7

Your student will grow up to be an adult one day. This is painfully obvious to parents. As they face adulthood, they will need to navigate a broken world. The Bible offers so many important things our student will need in adulthood. Things like moral guidance, courage, and hope. It is obvious why this is the first area we look. Without knowing the word of God, how can our students grow closer to Him? Where else can we see God's character, commands, and plans so clearly?

What scriptures does my child know?

Do they read/listen to the Bible during Bible time?

What Bible Stories do they know?

Things to think about when developing this goal:

1. How active am I in my daily Bible reading? Do I lead by example?
2. How can I help daily Bible reading become part of my student's routine?
3. How can I help my student relate to people in the Bible?
4. How can we make scripture interactive?
5. How can we use this to teach about accountability?

Prayer and Worship:

Then you will call on me and come and pray to me and I will listen to you. You will seek me and find me when you seek me with all your heart.

Jeremiah 29:12-13

Worship and prayer connect us to God. We talk about this almost every Sunday, but you cannot connect with the living God and not be changed. Worship changes things. Prayer changes things. There are so many things we want to see for our students. If it matters to your student, it probably matters to God. Whether they are praying to remember the things they studied in school or praising God for a new friend, prayer and worship need to be part of their lives, just like they need to be part of ours. Without them, people grow dull and faith begins to fall apart. Knowledge of the scripture is fantastic, but it means little without the next piece: relationship.

The starting point:

- Does my student pray?
- What things does my student include in prayer?
- Does my student know what worship is?
- Does my student recognize different ways to worship? (I.E. serving, singing)

Things to think about when developing this goal:

1. How active is worship in my relationship with God? Do I lead by example?
2. How can I help my kids find the places that they can actively serve?
3. Has my student been involved with prayer in our family?
4. Does he/she recognize how precious it is to be able to talk to God?
5. Do we make worship music a part of our home?

The Holy Spirit

There are different kinds of gifts, but the same Spirit distributes them. I Corinthians 12:4

The Holy Spirit is as active today as it was in the New Testament church. There are even specific mentions of the Holy Spirt in the Old Testament. People often have a hard time articulating exactly what the Holy Spirit does. Scripture tells us that the Holy Spirit is our advocate, that it reminds us of God's word, and that it gives us gifts. Everyone is gifted. Helping your student find their giftings will help them recognize how God works through them. This knowledge will encourage them to continue growing in the other areas.

The starting point:

- What does my student know about the Holy Spirit? (It's okay if the answer is nothing.)
- Does my student recognize the Holy Spirit's purpose/what He does?
- Does my student understand the different giftings the Holy Spirit gives to the church?

Things to think about:

1. Do I find this confusing? (There's no shame in not knowing. We just have to understand a concept to teach it effectively.)
2. What could my student's natural gifting of the Holy Spirit be?

Think back on moments where the Spirit was probably working in your student. Where they said something beyond their years, had peace in a scary situation, or where they boldly told someone about God. **Reflecting on what they have done/experienced can lead you on a path toward helping them discover their strengths and gifts.**

Goals:

Area 1 - Scripture memorization:
Goal:

_____
_____
_____

Area 2 – Prayer and Worship:
Goal:

_____
_____
_____

Area 3 – The Holy Spirit:
Goal:

_____
_____
_____

Communication Symbols

Break

Help

Drink

Bathroom

Stop

Hungry

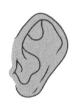

Listen

Wait

Yes

Sit

Too Loud

No

Game

Less

More

Bible

Pray

Play

Sing

Walk

All Done

No Touch

Communion

Kneel

Cold   Hot   Quiet

Safe   Tired   Sad

Go

Partnering with you:

I would love to partner with you and help however I can. Interested in help starting your special needs ministry—you got it. Just need someone who understands the unique struggles and joys this ministry brings – I am here. Just email me at accessiblegospel316@gmail.com

I also encourage you to contact Soar Special Needs Ministry. Their focus is empowering churches to do just what you have read about here: effectively support and empower our disabled brothers and sisters. Contact them at infor@soarspecialneeds.org

I would like to take a moment and write a special thank you to my friend, Sarah Stevens, who designed the images for me, and by extension, for you. Sweet Sarah, your hard work will help so many, may God bless you for your continued faithfulness.

Works Cited

Holy Bible: New Living Translation. Tyndale House Publishers, 2004.

McDaniel, Debbie. "40 Courageous Quotes from Evangelist Billy Graham." *Crosswalk.com*, Crosswalk.com, 21 Feb. 2018, https://www.crosswalk.com/faith/spiritual-life/inspiring-quotes/40-courageous-quotes-from-evangelist-billy-graham.html.

The Niv. Zondervan Bible Pub., 1983.

Crowns, Casting. "Casting Crowns - Start Right Here | Positive Encouraging K ..." *Start Right Here*, 2018, https://www.klove.com/music/artists/casting-crowns/start-right-here.

Media Relations, CDC. "CDC: 1 in 4 US Adults Live with a Disability." *Centers for Disease Control and Prevention*, Centers for Disease Control and Prevention, 16 Aug. 2018, https://www.cdc.gov/media/releases/2018/p0816-disability.html.

Grcevich MD, Stephen. "When Kids Become Aggressive at

Church." *Key Ministry*, Key Ministry, 17 Nov. 2016,

https://www.keyministry.org/church4everychild/2016/11

/17/when-kids-become-aggressive-at-

church?rq=aggressive.

Made in the USA
Columbia, SC
27 March 2022

58158933R00059